Die Katze Mit Den Tausend Leben: Zweisprachige Englisch-Deutsche Geschichten

My Pommeline

Published by My Pommeline, 2024.

While every precaution has been taken in the preparation of this book, the publisher assumes no responsibility for errors or omissions, or for damages resulting from the use of the information contained herein.

DIE KATZE MIT DEN TAUSEND LEBEN: ZWEISPRACHIGE ENGLISCH-DEUTSCHE GESCHICHTEN

First edition. October 14, 2024.

Copyright © 2024 My Pommeline.

ISBN: 979-8227009784

Written by My Pommeline.

Table of Contents

The Giant Pumpkin Parade

It was the morning after Halloween, and the small village of Muddington was unusually quiet. Streets that had been filled with children in costumes and glowing jack-o'-lanterns the night before were now littered with stray candy wrappers and drooping decorations.

But something strange was happening in Farmer McGregor's pumpkin patch just outside the village. One pumpkin, larger than all the rest, was starting to move. Its twisted stem wiggled, its orange skin gleamed in the early morning sunlight, and before anyone could notice, two triangular eyes carved themselves onto its surface. A wicked, lopsided grin followed.

The giant pumpkin had come to life.

The Pumpkin's Mischief Begins

Farmer McGregor had always been proud of his pumpkin patch, especially this year's prize-winning giant. But as he came out to check on his harvest that morning, he was in for a shock. His beloved pumpkin—his pride and joy—was rolling away!

"Hey! Where do you think you're going?" he shouted, stumbling over his boots as he tried to chase it.

But the mischievous pumpkin was faster than it looked. It rolled right through the fence, smashing the wooden posts as if they were twigs. Farmer McGregor tried to keep up, but the pumpkin bounced over the hill toward the village with a booming *thump, thump, thump*, leaving him gasping for breath.

In the village, Mrs. Crumble was sweeping her porch when the giant pumpkin came barreling down the street.

"Oh dear!" she cried, dropping her broom and barely leaping out of the way.

The pumpkin rolled past her, knocking over flowerpots, bouncing over benches, and sending a flock of chickens squawking in all directions. It crashed into a cart of apples, sending the fruit flying into the air like confetti. Children who were still groggy from last night's candy feast rubbed their eyes, wondering if they were seeing things.

The Pumpkin Parade

As the giant pumpkin rolled through the streets, more villagers began to gather, staring in disbelief. Soon, someone shouted, "It's alive!"

The pumpkin's carved grin grew wider as it rolled onto the village square. The mayor, Mr. Snodgrass, had just stepped out of his office, and his top hat went flying as the pumpkin zipped by.

"Stop that pumpkin!" he commanded, though he had no idea how anyone could stop such a massive, fast-moving fruit.

But the pumpkin wasn't done causing trouble. It rolled into the bakery, sending pies and loaves of bread flying out of the windows. Then it bounced toward the village green, where it scooped up a row of garden gnomes, carrying them along like tiny passengers on a parade float.

The villagers didn't know whether to laugh or scream. The pumpkin, growing ever more mischievous, began to spin in circles, dancing around the fountain, flinging water everywhere.

The Plan to Stop the Pumpkin

"We've got to stop it before it ruins the whole village!" cried Farmer McGregor, finally catching up with the crowd.

"But how do we stop a giant pumpkin?" asked Mrs. Crumble, who was still clutching her broom.

"Pumpkins don't like being smashed!" said young Tommy, a clever boy who loved reading about myths and monsters. "If we can make it crash into something, maybe it will stop!"

"But we can't just destroy it!" protested Farmer McGregor. "That's my prize pumpkin!"

The villagers huddled together, whispering and planning. Finally, Tommy came up with an idea.

"We'll lure it to the edge of the village," he said, "and get it to crash into the big pile of hay by the old barn! That way it won't be smashed, but it will stop."

"Brilliant!" said Mayor Snodgrass, adjusting his top hat. "Let's do it!"

The Pumpkin's Final Trick

Tommy grabbed a basket of the village's finest sweets and ran ahead, waving the candy in the air. "Hey, Pumpkin! Over here!"

The giant pumpkin, curious and greedy for more fun, followed Tommy as he zigzagged through the streets, its enormous orange body bouncing along behind him. The villagers cheered as Tommy led it straight toward the hay pile by the barn.

But just as they thought the plan was working, the pumpkin performed one last trick. It leaped into the air! Everyone gasped as it sailed over the haystack, spinning mid-air like a giant orange acrobat. It seemed certain the pumpkin would land and continue its chaos.

But instead, it bounced off the barn's roof and landed gently in the hay with a soft *thud*. Its grin slowly faded, its eyes dimmed, and it settled down, no longer rolling, no longer mischievous.

The village erupted into cheers.

A New Tradition

Farmer McGregor scratched his head as he approached the now peaceful pumpkin. "Well, I never thought I'd see the day when a pumpkin went on a parade," he said.

Tommy grinned. "Maybe we should make it a new tradition!"

Mayor Snodgrass smiled. "That's not a bad idea, young man. Next year, we'll have a proper Giant Pumpkin Parade—with pumpkins that *don't* roll away on their own, of course."

And so, the villagers of Muddington decided to honor their adventurous pumpkin with a yearly festival. Every November 1st, they would hold the Giant Pumpkin Parade, celebrating the mischievous pumpkin that caused havoc and brought the village together in a most unexpected way.

As for the giant pumpkin? It sat proudly on Farmer McGregor's farm until the next harvest, where it would return to its proper place in the parade—this time, safely on a float, not causing any more chaos.

But every now and then, if you looked closely, you could almost see its carved grin twitch, as if it was just waiting for its chance to roll free again.

Die Riesenkürbisparade

Es war der Morgen nach Halloween, und das kleine Dorf Muddington war ungewöhnlich ruhig. Die Straßen, die am Vorabend voller Kinder in Kostümen und leuchtenden Kürbislaternen gewesen waren, waren nun mit herumliegenden Süßigkeitenverpackungen und herunterhängenden Dekorationen übersät.

Aber etwas Seltsames geschah auf dem Kürbisfeld von Bauer McGregor, gleich außerhalb des Dorfes. Ein Kürbis, größer als alle anderen, begann sich zu bewegen. Sein verdrehter Stiel wackelte, seine orangefarbene Schale glänzte im morgendlichen Sonnenlicht, und bevor es jemand bemerken konnte, schnitzten sich zwei dreieckige Augen in seine Oberfläche. Ein böses, schiefes Grinsen folgte.

Der Riesenkürbis war zum Leben erwacht.

Der Kürbis beginnt seinen Schabernack

Bauer McGregor war immer stolz auf sein Kürbisfeld gewesen, besonders auf den riesigen Kürbis, der dieses Jahr den ersten Preis gewonnen hatte. Doch als er an diesem Morgen hinausging, um seine Ernte zu begutachten, erwartete ihn eine große Überraschung. Sein geliebter Kürbis—sein ganzer Stolz—rollte davon!

„Hey! Wo willst du hin?", rief er und stolperte über seine Stiefel, als er versuchte, ihn zu verfolgen.

Aber der schelmische Kürbis war schneller, als er aussah. Er rollte direkt durch den Zaun, wobei die Holzpfosten wie Zweige zerbrachen. Bauer McGregor versuchte mitzuhalten, aber der Kürbis hüpfte den Hügel hinunter in Richtung Dorf, mit einem dröhnenden *bum, bum, bum*, und ließ ihn keuchend zurück.

Im Dorf fegte Frau Crumble gerade ihre Veranda, als der riesige Kürbis die Straße hinunterrollte.

„Oh je!", rief sie, ließ ihren Besen fallen und sprang gerade noch rechtzeitig zur Seite.

Der Kürbis rollte an ihr vorbei, riss Blumentöpfe um, hüpfte über Bänke und jagte eine Schar Hühner in alle Richtungen. Er krachte in einen Apfelkarren, wodurch die Früchte wie Konfetti in die Luft flogen. Kinder, die noch benommen von den Süßigkeiten der letzten Nacht waren, rieben sich die Augen und fragten sich, ob sie träumten.

Die Kürbisparade

Während der Riesenkürbis durch die Straßen rollte, versammelten sich immer mehr Dorfbewohner und starrten ungläubig. Schließlich rief jemand: „Er lebt!"

Das geschnitzte Grinsen des Kürbisses wurde noch breiter, als er auf den Dorfplatz rollte. Der Bürgermeister, Herr Snodgrass, hatte gerade sein Büro verlassen, und sein Zylinder flog in die Luft, als der Kürbis an ihm vorbeizischte.

„Haltet diesen Kürbis auf!", befahl er, obwohl er keine Ahnung hatte, wie jemand solch eine riesige, schnell rollende Frucht aufhalten könnte.

Doch der Kürbis hatte noch nicht genug Unheil angerichtet. Er rollte in die Bäckerei und schleuderte Kuchen und Brotlaibe aus den Fenstern. Dann hüpfte er über den Dorfanger, wo er eine Reihe von Gartenzwergen einsammelte, die er wie kleine Passagiere auf einem Festwagen mit sich trug.

Die Dorfbewohner wussten nicht, ob sie lachen oder schreien sollten. Der Kürbis, der immer schelmischer wurde, begann sich im Kreis zu drehen, tanzte um den Brunnen herum und spritzte dabei Wasser in alle Richtungen.

Der Plan, den Kürbis zu stoppen

„Wir müssen ihn aufhalten, bevor er das ganze Dorf zerstört!", rief Bauer McGregor, der endlich bei der Menge angekommen war.

„Aber wie stoppen wir einen Riesenkürbis?", fragte Frau Crumble, die immer noch ihren Besen umklammerte.

„Kürbisse mögen es nicht, zerquetscht zu werden!", sagte der junge Tommy, ein schlauer Junge, der gerne Bücher über Mythen und Monster las. „Wenn wir ihn dazu bringen, gegen etwas zu krachen, hört er vielleicht auf!"

„Aber wir können ihn doch nicht einfach zerstören!", protestierte Bauer McGregor. „Das ist mein Preiskürbis!"

Die Dorfbewohner rückten zusammen, flüsterten und berieten sich. Schließlich hatte Tommy eine Idee.

„Wir locken ihn an den Rand des Dorfes", sagte er, „und lassen ihn gegen den großen Heuhaufen bei der alten Scheune krachen! So wird er nicht zerstört, aber er wird aufhören."

„Brillant!", sagte Bürgermeister Snodgrass und rückte seinen Zylinder zurecht. „Das machen wir!"

Der letzte Trick des Kürbisses

Tommy schnappte sich einen Korb mit den feinsten Süßigkeiten des Dorfes und rannte voraus, schwenkte die Süßigkeiten in der Luft. „Hey, Kürbis! Hier drüben!"

Der Riesenkürbis, neugierig und gierig nach mehr Spaß, folgte Tommy, der im Zickzack durch die Straßen rannte, während der riesige orangefarbene Kürbis ihm hinterherhüpfte. Die Dorfbewohner jubelten, als Tommy ihn direkt auf den Heuhaufen bei der Scheune zusteuerte.

Doch gerade als sie dachten, der Plan funktioniere, vollführte der Kürbis einen letzten Trick. Er sprang in die Luft! Alle schnauften vor Schreck, als er über den Heuhaufen segelte, sich in der Luft drehte wie ein riesiger orangefarbener Akrobat. Es sah so aus, als würde der Kürbis landen und weiter sein Chaos verbreiten.

Doch stattdessen prallte er vom Dach der Scheune ab und landete sanft im Heu mit einem leisen Plumps. Sein Grinsen verblasste langsam, seine Augen wurden dunkler, und er legte sich hin, rollte nicht mehr und war nicht mehr schelmisch.

Das Dorf brach in Jubel aus.

Eine neue Tradition

Bauer McGregor kratzte sich am Kopf, als er sich dem nun friedlichen Kürbis näherte. „Ich hätte nie gedacht, dass ich den Tag erlebe, an dem ein Kürbis auf Parade geht", sagte er.

Tommy grinste. „Vielleicht sollten wir daraus eine neue Tradition machen!"

Bürgermeister Snodgrass lächelte. „Das ist keine schlechte Idee, junger Mann. Nächstes Jahr machen wir eine richtige Riesenkürbisparade—mit Kürbissen, die nicht von alleine davonrollen, versteht sich."

Und so beschlossen die Dorfbewohner von Muddington, ihren abenteuerlustigen Kürbis mit einem jährlichen Fest zu ehren. Jedes Jahr am 1. November veranstalteten sie die Riesenkürbisparade und feierten den schelmischen Kürbis, der Chaos stiftete und das Dorf auf die unerwartetste Weise zusammenbrachte.

Und was den Riesenkürbis betrifft? Er saß stolz auf Bauer McGregors Hof bis zur nächsten Ernte, wo er wieder seinen Platz in der Parade einnehmen würde—diesmal sicher auf einem Festwagen, ohne weiteres Chaos zu stiften.

Aber hin und wieder, wenn man genau hinschaute, konnte man fast sehen, wie sein geschnitztes Grinsen zuckte, als ob er nur darauf wartete, wieder freizukommen.

The Boy Who Could Talk to Squirrels

In the small town of Oak Hollow, nestled between rolling hills and thick forests, lived a boy named Oliver. He was an ordinary boy in every way—ordinary height, ordinary hair, and ordinary shoes that squeaked a little when he walked. But Oliver had one secret, one thing that made him very extraordinary indeed: he could talk to squirrels.

It wasn't something he advertised, of course. People in Oak Hollow already thought Oliver was a bit odd, always hanging around trees and climbing them instead of playing football with the other boys. And while most kids went home after school to watch cartoons, Oliver went to the park and spent hours sitting under the big oak tree, quietly listening to the chittering sounds of his tiny, furry friends.

Oliver had discovered his special ability by accident when he was younger. One day, while playing in the woods, he found a baby squirrel trapped in a tangle of branches. As he reached out to help, the squirrel squeaked at him, and to his amazement, Oliver understood it perfectly.

"Help me! I'm stuck!" the squirrel had said.

From that moment on, Oliver could communicate with squirrels as easily as he could talk to humans—though squirrels were much more fun to talk to.

One crisp November morning, Oliver was walking to school when he noticed something strange. The squirrels in Oak Hollow seemed... frantic. Normally, they would be gathering nuts, darting up and down trees, and chatting about their day. But today, they were all running around wildly, squeaking in panic.

Oliver crouched down near the base of a large oak tree where a particularly plump squirrel named Nutty was hopping nervously from branch to branch.

"Nutty! What's going on?" Oliver called up.

Nutty leaped down and ran over to him, his tiny paws trembling. "It's terrible, Oliver! The humans—they're planning to cut down the trees!"

Oliver's heart sank. "What do you mean? Why would they do that?"

Nutty's tail twitched furiously. "I overheard some men in suits talking near the park. They said they want to build more houses, and the first thing they're going to do is chop down all the trees!"

Oliver couldn't believe what he was hearing. The trees of Oak Hollow were ancient and beautiful, towering over the town like silent guardians. The squirrels, birds, and countless other creatures made their homes there. Not to mention, the trees gave Oak Hollow its name!

"Are you sure, Nutty?" Oliver asked, hoping there had been some mistake.

Nutty nodded sadly. "They're starting tomorrow. The trees are in danger, Oliver. You have to help us!"

The Plan to Save the Trees

Oliver knew he had to act fast. But what could a boy like him do to stop grown-ups from chopping down the trees? As he walked to school, his mind raced. He couldn't let this happen—he had to come up with a plan. By the time he arrived at class, Oliver had an idea, and it was just crazy enough to work.

During lunch, Oliver gathered his friends, Mila and Jacob, who always helped him when he needed it. "Listen," he said in a low voice, "I need your help with something really important."

Mila raised an eyebrow. "What kind of important? Is it like the time you wanted us to dig for buried treasure in the park?"

"No, this is bigger," Oliver replied. "The town's going to cut down the trees. All of them. We have to stop them."

Jacob looked skeptical. "And how do you plan to do that? The mayor's the one making those decisions, and last I checked, she wasn't afraid of kids."

Oliver grinned. "No, but she might listen to squirrels."

"Squirrels?" Mila and Jacob exchanged confused looks.

"Trust me," Oliver said, leaning in closer. "I can talk to squirrels. I've been able to for years."

His friends stared at him in disbelief. "Are you serious?" Mila asked, half-laughing.

"Completely," Oliver said. "And I've got a plan. We're going to gather all the squirrels in Oak Hollow, and we're going to show the town why these trees matter—by making sure the squirrels tell their side of the story."

The Squirrel Army

That afternoon, instead of going home, Oliver and his friends went to the park. With a quick whistle, Oliver called out, and within moments, squirrels began to appear from every tree, bush, and crevice. Dozens of them, from Nutty to Peanut to a particularly energetic little one named Twitch.

Oliver explained the situation to his furry friends, and the squirrels listened intently.

"We'll do anything to save our homes," said Peanut, his whiskers twitching.

"Good," said Oliver. "Here's what we're going to do..."

Over the next few hours, Oliver and his friends put their plan into action. The squirrels would sneak into the town meeting that night, where the mayor would be discussing the new housing plans. But they wouldn't just sit quietly—they were going to cause a scene. A big one.

The Squirrels Take a Stand

That evening, the mayor of Oak Hollow, Mayor Price, stood before the gathered crowd at the town hall. She was talking about the benefits of expanding the town, and how the new houses would bring more people and more business.

But just as she began to show a map of where the trees would be cut down, a commotion broke out. A furry ball of energy shot across the room—Twitch, the energetic squirrel, darted under chairs, squeaking loudly.

"What's that? A squirrel?" someone yelled.

Then, from every corner of the room, more squirrels appeared—Nutty, Peanut, and their entire crew. They chittered and chirped, leaping onto tables, knocking over papers, and running up people's legs. The room erupted in chaos as the mayor tried to calm everyone down.

"What's going on?" Mayor Price shouted over the noise.

Suddenly, Oliver stood up. "Wait!" he called out. The room quieted as the squirrels paused their rampage. "These squirrels are trying to tell us something!"

The mayor looked at him, bewildered. "Squirrels... trying to tell us something?"

Oliver nodded. "They live in those trees. Cutting them down would destroy their homes. They can't speak for themselves, but I can."

The mayor blinked. "You... can talk to squirrels?"

Oliver nodded confidently. "And they don't want their trees to be destroyed. Neither do the birds or the other animals. We need the trees. We need them for the fresh air, for the shade, and for the beauty they bring to Oak Hollow."

The crowd murmured. Even the mayor seemed to soften as she looked around the room, now filled with the pleading eyes of dozens of squirrels.

A New Decision

After a long pause, Mayor Price finally sighed. "Well, I didn't expect to be negotiating with squirrels today," she said, a hint of a smile on her face. "But you're right, Oliver. We need to protect our trees. Maybe we can find another place for the houses."

The room erupted in applause. The squirrels chittered happily, scampering around in victory. Oliver grinned and gave Nutty a thumbs-up.

A Hero for the Trees

From that day on, Oliver became known as the boy who saved Oak Hollow's trees. The townspeople respected him, not just for his bravery, but for reminding them of the importance of nature. And the squirrels? Well, they continued to chat with Oliver every day, their homes safe and sound in the tall, towering oaks that stood proudly over the village.

Der Junge, der mit Eichhörnchen sprechen konnte

In der kleinen Stadt Oak Hollow, eingebettet zwischen sanften Hügeln und dichten Wäldern, lebte ein Junge namens Oliver. Er war in jeder Hinsicht ein ganz normaler Junge – normale Größe, normales Haar und normale Schuhe, die ein wenig quietschten, wenn er ging. Aber Oliver hatte ein Geheimnis, etwas, das ihn sehr außergewöhnlich machte: Er konnte mit Eichhörnchen sprechen.

Natürlich erzählte er das niemandem. Die Leute in Oak Hollow hielten Oliver ohnehin schon für ein bisschen seltsam, weil er immer in der Nähe von Bäumen herumhing und auf sie kletterte, anstatt mit den anderen Jungs Fußball zu spielen. Während die meisten Kinder nach der Schule nach Hause gingen, um Zeichentrickfilme zu schauen, ging Oliver in den Park und verbrachte Stunden unter der großen Eiche, lauschte leise den quirligen Geräuschen seiner kleinen, pelzigen Freunde.

Oliver hatte seine besondere Fähigkeit zufällig entdeckt, als er noch jünger war. Eines Tages, als er im Wald spielte, fand er ein Baby-Eichhörnchen, das sich in einem Zweiggewirr verfangen hatte. Als er die Hand ausstreckte, um zu helfen, quiekte das Eichhörnchen, und zu Olivers Erstaunen verstand er es perfekt.

„Hilf mir! Ich stecke fest!", hatte das Eichhörnchen gesagt.

Von diesem Moment an konnte Oliver genauso leicht mit Eichhörnchen kommunizieren wie mit Menschen – obwohl es viel mehr Spaß machte, mit Eichhörnchen zu sprechen.

Die Bedrohung in Oak Hollow

Eines frischen Novembermorgens ging Oliver zur Schule, als er etwas Merkwürdiges bemerkte. Die Eichhörnchen in Oak Hollow schienen... aufgeregt. Normalerweise sammelten sie Nüsse, huschten die Bäume rauf und runter und plauderten über ihren Tag. Aber heute rannten sie alle wild herum und quiekten panisch.

Oliver hockte sich in der Nähe einer großen Eiche nieder, wo ein besonders dickes Eichhörnchen namens Nutty nervös von Ast zu Ast sprang.

„Nutty! Was ist los?", rief Oliver hinauf.

Nutty sprang hinunter und rannte zu ihm, seine kleinen Pfoten zitterten. „Es ist schrecklich, Oliver! Die Menschen – sie planen, die Bäume zu fällen!"

Olivers Herz sank. „Was meinst du? Warum sollten sie das tun?"

Nutties Schwanz zuckte heftig. „Ich habe einige Männer in Anzügen im Park belauscht. Sie haben gesagt, sie wollen mehr Häuser bauen, und das Erste, was sie tun werden, ist, alle Bäume zu fällen!"

Oliver konnte nicht fassen, was er da hörte. Die Bäume von Oak Hollow waren uralt und wunderschön, sie überragten die Stadt wie stille Wächter. Die Eichhörnchen, Vögel und unzählige andere Tiere machten dort ihre Heimat. Ganz zu schweigen davon, dass die Bäume Oak Hollow seinen Namen gaben!

„Bist du sicher, Nutty?", fragte Oliver und hoffte, dass es ein Missverständnis war.

Nutty nickte traurig. „Sie fangen morgen an. Die Bäume sind in Gefahr, Oliver. Du musst uns helfen!"

Der Plan, die Bäume zu retten

Oliver wusste, dass er schnell handeln musste. Aber was könnte ein Junge wie er tun, um Erwachsene davon abzuhalten, die Bäume zu fällen? Auf dem Weg zur Schule rasten seine Gedanken. Er konnte das nicht zulassen – er musste einen Plan schmieden. Als er in der Schule ankam, hatte Oliver eine Idee, und sie war verrückt genug, um zu funktionieren.

Während des Mittagessens versammelte Oliver seine Freunde, Mila und Jacob, die ihm immer halfen, wenn er sie brauchte. „Hört zu", sagte er leise, „ich brauche eure Hilfe bei etwas wirklich Wichtigem."

Mila hob eine Augenbraue. „Was für wichtig? Ist es wie damals, als du uns überreden wolltest, im Park nach vergrabenen Schätzen zu graben?"

„Nein, das hier ist größer", antwortete Oliver. „Die Stadt will die Bäume fällen. Alle. Wir müssen sie aufhalten."

Jacob sah skeptisch aus. „Und wie willst du das anstellen? Der Bürgermeister trifft diese Entscheidungen, und soweit ich weiß, hat sie keine Angst vor Kindern."

Oliver grinste. „Nein, aber vielleicht hört sie auf Eichhörnchen."

„Eichhörnchen?", Mila und Jacob tauschten verwirrte Blicke aus.

„Vertraut mir", sagte Oliver und beugte sich näher. „Ich kann mit Eichhörnchen sprechen. Schon seit Jahren."

Seine Freunde starrten ihn ungläubig an. „Im Ernst?", fragte Mila halb lachend.

„Völlig", sagte Oliver. „Und ich habe einen Plan. Wir werden alle Eichhörnchen in Oak Hollow versammeln, und wir werden der Stadt zeigen, warum diese Bäume wichtig sind – indem wir sicherstellen, dass die Eichhörnchen ihre Geschichte erzählen."

Die Eichhörnchen-Armee

An diesem Nachmittag gingen Oliver und seine Freunde nicht nach Hause, sondern in den Park. Mit einem kurzen Pfiff rief Oliver, und innerhalb weniger Augenblicke erschienen Eichhörnchen aus jedem Baum, Busch und jeder Spalte. Dutzende von ihnen, von Nutty über Peanut bis hin zu einem besonders energiegeladenen kleinen Eichhörnchen namens Twitch.

Oliver erklärte die Situation seinen pelzigen Freunden, und die Eichhörnchen hörten aufmerksam zu.

„Wir tun alles, um unsere Heimat zu retten", sagte Peanut, seine Schnurrhaare zitterten.

„Gut", sagte Oliver. „Hier ist der Plan..."

In den nächsten Stunden setzten Oliver und seine Freunde ihren Plan in die Tat um. Die Eichhörnchen würden sich heimlich in die Stadtratssitzung schleichen, die an diesem Abend stattfand, wo der Bürgermeister die neuen Baupläne besprechen würde. Aber sie würden nicht still dasitzen – sie würden einen großen Aufruhr veranstalten. Einen gewaltigen.

Die Eichhörnchen erheben sich

An diesem Abend stand die Bürgermeisterin von Oak Hollow, Bürgermeisterin Price, vor der versammelten Menge im Rathaus. Sie sprach über die Vorteile der Stadterweiterung und wie die neuen Häuser mehr Menschen und mehr Geschäft bringen würden.

Doch gerade als sie begann, eine Karte zu zeigen, auf der die Bäume gefällt werden sollten, brach plötzlich ein Tumult aus. Eine pelzige Energiekugel sauste durch den Raum – Twitch, das energiegeladene Eichhörnchen, huschte unter den Stühlen hindurch und quiekte laut.

„Was ist das? Ein Eichhörnchen?", rief jemand.

Dann tauchten aus jeder Ecke des Raumes weitere Eichhörnchen auf – Nutty, Peanut und ihre ganze Bande. Sie quiekten und zirpten, sprangen auf Tische, warfen Papiere um und liefen den Menschen an den Beinen hoch. Der Raum brach in Chaos aus, während die Bürgermeisterin versuchte, die Menge zu beruhigen.

„Was ist hier los?", rief Bürgermeisterin Price über den Lärm hinweg.

Plötzlich stand Oliver auf. „Wartet!", rief er. Der Raum wurde leiser, als die Eichhörnchen ihre Rampage unterbrachen. „Diese Eichhörnchen versuchen, uns etwas zu sagen!"

Die Bürgermeisterin sah ihn verwirrt an. „Eichhörnchen... versuchen, uns etwas zu sagen?"

Oliver nickte. „Sie leben in diesen Bäumen. Wenn wir sie fällen, zerstören wir ihre Heimat. Sie können nicht für sich selbst sprechen, aber ich kann es."

Die Bürgermeisterin blinzelte. „Du... kannst mit Eichhörnchen sprechen?"

Oliver nickte selbstbewusst. „Und sie wollen nicht, dass ihre Bäume zerstört werden. Auch die Vögel und anderen Tiere nicht. Wir brauchen die Bäume. Wir brauchen sie für die frische Luft, den Schatten und die Schönheit, die sie Oak Hollow bringen."

Die Menge murmelte. Sogar die Bürgermeisterin schien nachzugeben, als sie sich im Raum umsah, der nun von den flehenden Augen Dutzender Eichhörnchen erfüllt war.

Eine neue Entscheidung

Nach einer langen Pause seufzte Bürgermeisterin Price schließlich. „Nun, ich hätte nicht erwartet, heute mit Eichhörnchen zu verhandeln", sagte sie mit einem Hauch eines Lächelns im Gesicht. „Aber du hast recht, Oliver. Wir müssen unsere Bäume schützen. Vielleicht finden wir einen anderen Platz für die Häuser."

Der Raum brach in Applaus aus. Die Eichhörnchen quiekten glücklich und sprangen siegestrunken umher. Oliver grinste und zeigte Nutty den Daumen nach oben.

Ein Held für die Bäume

Von diesem Tag an war Oliver als der Junge bekannt, der die Bäume von Oak Hollow gerettet hatte. Die Stadtbewohner respektierten ihn nicht nur für seinen Mut, sondern auch dafür, dass er sie an die Bedeutung der Natur erinnerte. Und die Eichhörnchen? Nun, sie plauderten weiterhin jeden Tag mit Oliver, ihre Heimat sicher und wohlbehalten in den hohen, majestätischen Eichen, die stolz über dem Dorf standen.

The Girl Who Turned Invisible at School

———

In the bustling corridors of Willowbrook Primary, there was a girl named Ivy who felt like she barely existed. While everyone else chatted, laughed, and shared stories during lunch breaks, Ivy preferred to stay quiet, tucked away in the corner with her sketchbook. She wasn't unfriendly; she just felt... invisible.

No one ever picked her for games during PE, and during group projects, she was always the one who sat silently while the others talked over her. The teachers were kind, but they didn't really notice her either, apart from a gentle "Are you okay, Ivy?" once in a while. Ivy wished that, for once, someone would see her—not just her face, but *really* see who she was. But deep down, she also wished she could disappear completely, blending into the background like she already felt she did.

One Monday morning, Ivy got her wish—just not in the way she expected.

A Strange Discovery

It started in the middle of a history lesson, as Ivy stared at her hands while Ms. Baxter explained the rise and fall of ancient empires. Ivy always found history fascinating, but today, her mind wandered to how she was going to get through another lunch break by herself. She let out a small sigh and gazed down at her hands, which were resting on her desk.

And then she noticed something strange. Her hands... were fading.

Ivy blinked and rubbed her eyes. Maybe she was just tired? But no—the more she looked, the more her hands seemed to be disappearing, like mist dissolving into the air. Startled, she raised her arm to show Ms. Baxter, but her entire arm had faded away, too!

She froze. This wasn't just in her imagination—she was actually turning invisible!

Ivy looked around the room. No one seemed to notice. Ms. Baxter kept droning on about ancient warriors, and her classmates continued passing notes, doodling in their notebooks, or staring blankly at the board.

For the first time in her life, Ivy was truly invisible.

An Invisible Day

At first, it was terrifying. Ivy didn't know what to do. She cautiously stood up from her desk and moved toward the door, half-expecting someone to call out, "Hey, where are you going?" But no one said a word. She was invisible, and apparently, unnoticed.

As she slipped out of the classroom, a strange thrill coursed through her. No one could see her! She could go anywhere, do anything, and no one would even know. Maybe being invisible wasn't so bad after all.

For the rest of the day, Ivy wandered the halls of Willowbrook Primary, marveling at her new ability. She walked straight past the teachers without worrying about getting into trouble. She entered the cafeteria without needing to line up for food and even took a peek inside the teachers' lounge, where Ms. Baxter was drinking coffee and discussing something Ivy couldn't hear.

During lunch, she sat at the most popular table, right next to the girls who normally ignored her, and they didn't even glance in her direction. She could hear their gossip, their giggles, but not a single word they said mattered anymore. Ivy smiled to herself. She didn't need their approval. She was invisible, and for once, she liked it.

The Problem with Invisibility

By the end of the school day, Ivy had grown more comfortable with her newfound power. But as the afternoon wore on, a strange feeling began to creep into her chest. At first, being invisible had felt like a superpower, a way to escape the loneliness she had always felt. But now, it was starting to feel different. As she walked the halls, completely unseen, she realized that no one—not a single person—had even noticed she was missing.

There was no, *"Hey, where's Ivy?"* or *"I haven't seen Ivy all day!"* She had disappeared, and it seemed like no one cared.

Ivy frowned. The thrill of invisibility was starting to wear off. What was the point of being invisible if no one ever missed you when you were gone?

By the time the final bell rang, Ivy was standing outside the school, watching everyone leave. She saw her classmates walk out in groups, chatting and laughing as if nothing was out of the ordinary. Her heart sank. What if she stayed invisible forever? Would anyone even remember she had ever existed?

A New Realization

That night, Ivy sat alone in her room, still invisible and unsure what to do. She stared at her reflection—or rather, the lack of one—in the mirror. She thought about how she had spent her day wandering around, unnoticed, and how at first, it had been fun. But now, all she wanted was to be seen again.

As she lay down in bed, a thought occurred to her. Maybe it wasn't the world that needed to see her differently. Maybe it was *her* who needed to see herself differently. All this time, she had been waiting for someone else to notice her, to make her feel like she mattered. But what if she didn't need their approval to stand out?

Maybe, just maybe, the key to being seen wasn't about blending in or being invisible. Maybe it was about standing out in her own way, being brave enough to show the world who she really was—even if it scared her.

With that thought in her mind, Ivy closed her eyes and drifted off to sleep.

The Next Day

The next morning, when Ivy woke up, the first thing she did was look at her hands. They were visible again! She could see the familiar freckle on her right hand and the scar on her left thumb from when she had fallen off her bike years ago.

Ivy smiled. She was back.

But something had changed. Not just her visibility, but something deeper. Today, she wasn't going to hide in the background. She wasn't going to let her shyness make her feel invisible anymore.

At school, Ivy walked confidently into her classroom. She smiled at Ms. Baxter, who smiled back. Instead of slipping into her usual seat at the back, Ivy sat near the front. When the teacher asked a question, Ivy raised her hand—something she had never done before.

Ms. Baxter looked pleasantly surprised. "Yes, Ivy?"

Ivy answered the question, her voice clear and steady. She noticed a few of her classmates glance her way in surprise, but she didn't care. For the first time, Ivy felt like she truly belonged in that room.

At lunch, instead of sitting alone in the corner, Ivy approached a group of kids and asked if she could sit with them. They nodded, and soon, they were chatting about school, their favorite books, and what they liked to do after class.

Ivy realized something important that day: she didn't need invisibility to feel safe. She didn't need to blend in or hide. She just needed to believe in herself—and when she did, the world started to notice her, too.

From that day forward, Ivy was still quiet, still shy at times, but she wasn't invisible. She made friends, spoke up in class, and started showing her drawings to her classmates, who were impressed by her talent. The more she embraced who she was, the more people noticed her—not because she tried to be like everyone else, but because she was herself.

And as for the invisibility? It never returned. But Ivy didn't mind. She had learned how to stand out all on her own.

Das Mädchen, das in der Schule unsichtbar wurde

In den belebten Fluren der Willowbrook-Grundschule gab es ein Mädchen namens Ivy, das sich fühlte, als ob sie kaum existierte. Während alle anderen redeten, lachten und in den Pausen Geschichten austauschten, zog es Ivy vor, still zu bleiben und sich mit ihrem Skizzenbuch in eine Ecke zurückzuziehen. Sie war nicht unfreundlich, sie fühlte sich nur... unsichtbar.

Niemand wählte sie jemals für Spiele im Sportunterricht, und bei Gruppenarbeiten war sie immer diejenige, die schweigend dasaß, während die anderen über sie hinweg redeten. Die Lehrer waren freundlich, aber sie bemerkten sie auch nicht wirklich, abgesehen von einem gelegentlichen „Geht es dir gut, Ivy?". Ivy wünschte sich, dass sie einmal jemand sehen würde – nicht nur ihr Gesicht, sondern wirklich sehen würde, wer sie war. Doch tief im Inneren wünschte sie sich auch, vollständig zu verschwinden, um mit dem Hintergrund zu verschmelzen, so wie sie sich bereits fühlte.

Eines Montagmorgens erfüllte sich Ivys Wunsch – nur nicht so, wie sie es erwartet hatte.

Eine seltsame Entdeckung

Es begann mitten im Geschichtsunterricht, als Ivy auf ihre Hände starrte, während Frau Baxter den Aufstieg und Fall antiker Reiche erklärte. Ivy fand Geschichte immer faszinierend, aber heute schweiften ihre Gedanken ab und sie überlegte, wie sie die nächste Mittagspause wieder allein überstehen würde. Sie seufzte leise und blickte auf ihre Hände, die auf ihrem Schreibtisch ruhten.

Und dann bemerkte sie etwas Seltsames. Ihre Hände... verschwanden.

Ivy blinzelte und rieb sich die Augen. Vielleicht war sie einfach nur müde? Aber nein – je länger sie hinsah, desto mehr schienen ihre Hände zu verblassen, wie Nebel, der sich in Luft auflöst. Erschrocken hob sie ihren Arm, um Frau Baxter zu zeigen, was geschah, aber auch ihr ganzer Arm war verschwunden!

Sie erstarrte. Das war nicht nur Einbildung – sie wurde wirklich unsichtbar!

Ivy blickte sich im Raum um. Niemand schien es zu bemerken. Frau Baxter redete weiter über alte Krieger, und ihre Mitschüler schrieben Zettelchen, kritzelten in ihre Notizbücher oder starrten gelangweilt auf die Tafel.

Zum ersten Mal in ihrem Leben war Ivy wirklich unsichtbar.

Ein unsichtbarer Tag

Zuerst war es erschreckend. Ivy wusste nicht, was sie tun sollte. Vorsichtig stand sie von ihrem Schreibtisch auf und ging zur Tür, halb erwartend, dass jemand rufen würde: „Hey, wo gehst du hin?" Aber niemand sagte ein Wort. Sie war unsichtbar und offenbar unbemerkt.

Als sie aus dem Klassenzimmer schlich, durchfuhr sie ein seltsames Kribbeln. Niemand konnte sie sehen! Sie konnte überall hingehen, alles tun, und niemand würde es merken. Vielleicht war es gar nicht so schlecht, unsichtbar zu sein.

Den Rest des Tages verbrachte Ivy damit, durch die Flure der Willowbrook-Grundschule zu wandern und ihre neue Fähigkeit zu bestaunen. Sie ging direkt an den Lehrern vorbei, ohne sich Sorgen zu machen, Ärger zu bekommen. Sie betrat die Cafeteria, ohne sich für das Essen anzustellen, und warf sogar einen Blick in das Lehrerzimmer, wo Frau Baxter Kaffee trank und über etwas sprach, das Ivy nicht hören konnte.

Während des Mittagessens saß sie am beliebtesten Tisch, direkt neben den Mädchen, die sie sonst immer ignorierten, und sie warfen keinen einzigen Blick in ihre Richtung. Sie hörte ihr Getratsche und ihr Kichern, aber kein einziges Wort davon war für sie von Bedeutung. Ivy lächelte in sich hinein. Sie brauchte ihre Anerkennung nicht. Sie war unsichtbar, und zum ersten Mal gefiel ihr das.

Das Problem mit der Unsichtbarkeit

Gegen Ende des Schultages fühlte sich Ivy zunehmend wohler mit ihrer neuen Fähigkeit. Aber je weiter der Nachmittag fortschritt, desto mehr schlich sich ein seltsames Gefühl in ihre Brust. Zuerst hatte sich die Unsichtbarkeit wie eine Superkraft angefühlt, eine Möglichkeit, der Einsamkeit zu entkommen, die sie immer gespürt hatte. Doch nun begann es, sich anders anzufühlen. Als sie durch die Flure ging, völlig unbemerkt, wurde ihr klar, dass niemand – wirklich niemand – bemerkt hatte, dass sie fehlte.

Es gab kein „Hey, wo ist Ivy?" oder „Ich habe Ivy den ganzen Tag nicht gesehen!" Sie war verschwunden, und es schien, als ob es niemanden kümmerte.

Ivy runzelte die Stirn. Der Nervenkitzel der Unsichtbarkeit begann zu verblassen. Was nützte es, unsichtbar zu sein, wenn niemand einen vermisste, wenn man weg war?

Als die Schulglocke am Ende des Tages läutete, stand Ivy draußen und beobachtete, wie alle nach Hause gingen. Sie sah ihre Mitschüler in Gruppen herauskommen, lachend und plaudernd, als wäre nichts Ungewöhnliches passiert. Ihr Herz sank. Was, wenn sie für immer unsichtbar blieb? Würde sich überhaupt jemand daran erinnern, dass sie je existiert hatte?

Eine neue Erkenntnis

An diesem Abend saß Ivy allein in ihrem Zimmer, noch immer unsichtbar und unsicher, was sie tun sollte. Sie starrte in den Spiegel – oder besser gesagt, in das, was sie nicht sah. Sie dachte darüber nach, wie sie ihren Tag damit verbracht hatte, unbemerkt herumzuwandern, und wie das zuerst Spaß gemacht hatte. Doch jetzt wollte sie nichts mehr, als wieder gesehen zu werden.

Als sie sich ins Bett legte, kam ihr ein Gedanke. Vielleicht war es nicht die Welt, die sie anders sehen musste. Vielleicht musste sie sich selbst anders sehen. Die ganze Zeit hatte sie darauf gewartet, dass jemand sie bemerkt, ihr das Gefühl gibt, dass sie wichtig ist.

Aber was, wenn sie gar nicht deren Zustimmung brauchte, um aufzufallen?

Vielleicht, nur vielleicht, lag der Schlüssel dazu, gesehen zu werden, nicht darin, sich anzupassen oder unsichtbar zu sein. Vielleicht ging es darum, auf ihre eigene Art aufzufallen und mutig genug zu sein, der Welt zu zeigen, wer sie wirklich war – selbst wenn es sie erschreckte.

Mit diesem Gedanken schlief Ivy ein.

Der nächste Tag

Am nächsten Morgen, als Ivy aufwachte, schaute sie als Erstes auf ihre Hände. Sie waren wieder sichtbar! Sie konnte den vertrauten Leberfleck auf ihrer rechten Hand und die Narbe auf ihrem linken Daumen sehen, die sie sich vor Jahren zugezogen hatte, als sie vom Fahrrad gefallen war.

Ivy lächelte. Sie war zurück.

Aber etwas hatte sich verändert. Nicht nur ihre Sichtbarkeit, sondern etwas Tieferes. Heute würde sie sich nicht mehr im Hintergrund verstecken. Sie würde nicht mehr zulassen, dass ihre Schüchternheit sie unsichtbar machte.

In der Schule ging Ivy selbstbewusst in ihr Klassenzimmer. Sie lächelte Frau Baxter an, die zurücklächelte. Anstatt sich wie üblich in die hintere Reihe zu setzen, nahm Ivy einen Platz weiter vorne. Als die Lehrerin eine Frage stellte, hob Ivy die Hand – etwas, das sie noch nie zuvor getan hatte.

Frau Baxter sah angenehm überrascht aus. „Ja, Ivy?"

Ivy beantwortete die Frage, ihre Stimme war klar und ruhig. Einige ihrer Mitschüler warfen ihr überraschte Blicke zu, aber das war ihr egal. Zum ersten Mal fühlte sich Ivy, als gehöre sie wirklich in diesen Raum.

In der Mittagspause, anstatt allein in der Ecke zu sitzen, ging Ivy auf eine Gruppe Kinder zu und fragte, ob sie sich dazusetzen könne. Sie nickten, und bald unterhielten sie sich über die Schule, ihre Lieblingsbücher und darüber, was sie nach dem Unterricht gerne machten.

An diesem Tag erkannte Ivy etwas Wichtiges: Sie brauchte keine Unsichtbarkeit, um sich sicher zu fühlen. Sie musste nicht hineinpassen oder sich verstecken. Sie musste nur an sich selbst glauben – und als sie das tat, begann die Welt, sie auch zu bemerken.

Ein neuer Anfang

Von diesem Tag an war Ivy immer noch ruhig, manchmal immer noch schüchtern, aber sie war nicht mehr unsichtbar. Sie fand Freunde, meldete sich im Unterricht und begann, ihren Mitschülern ihre Zeichnungen zu zeigen, die sie beeindruckten. Je mehr sie sich selbst annahm, desto mehr bemerkten die Leute sie – nicht, weil sie versuchte, wie alle anderen zu sein, sondern weil sie sie selbst war.

Und was die Unsichtbarkeit betraf? Sie kehrte nie zurück. Aber das störte Ivy nicht. Sie hatte gelernt, ganz allein aufzufallen.

The Great Underwater Treasure Hunt

Tommy and Max had always been best friends. They lived in a seaside village where the salty breeze carried the scent of adventure, and their imaginations ran as wild as the crashing waves. Every day after school, they would meet at the beach and dream about the hidden mysteries beneath the sea.

One Saturday morning, something extraordinary happened that would turn their wildest dreams into reality.

The Discovery

It was a bright, sunny day when Tommy and Max went out to explore the tide pools near the rocky cliffs. They had done this a hundred times before, searching for crabs, shiny shells, and tiny fish, but today felt different. As they scrambled over the slippery rocks, Tommy's foot kicked something hard.

"Ow!" Tommy winced, rubbing his foot.

"What's that?" Max asked, pointing at the shiny object half-buried in the sand.

Tommy crouched down and dug it out. It was an old, rusted metal box. The hinges were creaky, and the surface was covered in strange markings. Max's eyes widened as Tommy carefully pried the box open.

Inside, they found a rolled-up piece of parchment, yellowed with age. Max unrolled it, and their hearts raced. It was an ancient treasure map! The markings looked like they were centuries old, and the map showed a route leading far out into the sea, marked by a giant 'X'.

"Tommy, do you know what this means?" Max whispered, his voice trembling with excitement.

Tommy grinned. "It means we're going on a treasure hunt!"

Planning the Adventure

That afternoon, the boys met at their secret clubhouse—a treehouse in Tommy's backyard. They spread the map out on the floor, examining every detail. The route began at their village beach and stretched far into the deep blue ocean, past a coral reef and an underwater cave.

"We're going to need diving gear," Max said.

"And a boat!" Tommy added.

Luckily, Tommy's dad had a small fishing boat, and Max's older sister worked at the local scuba diving shop. The boys spent the rest of the day preparing for their grand adventure. They borrowed diving suits, snorkels, and packed their bags with snacks and supplies.

By the time the sun began to set, they were ready.

"We'll set out at dawn," Tommy said, his voice brimming with anticipation.

Max nodded. "Tomorrow, we'll find the treasure."

Setting Sail

The next morning, with the first light of day, Tommy and Max loaded their gear onto the small boat and set off. The water shimmered like liquid gold under the rising sun, and the boys felt a sense of excitement bubbling inside them.

They followed the map's route, navigating the coastline until they reached the coral reef. Brightly colored fish swam beneath them, darting between the rocks and coral. The reef was breathtaking, but the boys had something much bigger on their minds: treasure.

"According to the map, the entrance to the underwater cave is just beyond the reef," Tommy said, squinting at the parchment.

Max scanned the horizon. "There! I see it!" He pointed to a dark shape below the surface.

They anchored the boat and suited up in their diving gear. With their hearts pounding in their chests, the boys plunged into the cool water. As they swam down, the world above them disappeared, replaced by a magical underwater kingdom.

The Underwater Cave

The entrance to the cave was massive, a yawning mouth in the ocean floor. The boys swam inside, their flashlights cutting through the darkness. The cave was eerie but beautiful. Glittering stones lined the walls, and strange sea creatures peeked out from hidden nooks.

Tommy pointed ahead. "There it is—the 'X'!"

In the center of the cave, carved into the rocky floor, was a giant 'X', just like on the map.

Max's eyes widened. "This is it!"

They swam down to the 'X' and began searching for any clues. Max's hand brushed against something metallic. He cleared away the sand, revealing a large, ancient chest covered in barnacles.

"Help me lift it!" Max called, excitement and effort in his voice.

Together, they heaved the chest out of the sand. It was heavy, but the promise of what lay inside fueled their strength. Tommy pried the chest open with a crowbar, and their eyes widened as they gazed at its contents.

The Treasure

The chest was filled with sparkling gold coins, glittering jewels, and intricately carved statues. There were ancient relics of lost civilizations and even a crown encrusted with diamonds. It was more treasure than they could have ever imagined.

"We're rich!" Tommy shouted, his voice bubbling through his snorkel.

Max laughed. "This is amazing! We've really found a hidden treasure!"

But as they admired their discovery, they noticed something else at the bottom of the chest—a rolled-up piece of parchment, similar to the map they had found earlier. Max unrolled it, and the boys stared in disbelief.

It was another treasure map.

"But this one is even further away," Tommy said, examining the new map. It showed a route leading even deeper into the ocean, to a place they had never seen before.

Max grinned. "Looks like our adventure isn't over yet."

A Grand Return

After taking what they could carry, the boys returned to their boat, hearts full of excitement. As they sailed back to shore, they couldn't stop grinning. They had found real treasure, and the adventure of a lifetime wasn't over yet.

When they reached the beach, they shared their story with their families. Of course, the adults didn't believe them at first—until they showed them the glittering gold coins and jewels.

Tommy's dad raised an eyebrow. "You boys sure know how to find trouble," he said, smiling. "But it looks like you've also found an adventure of a lifetime."

Max's sister ruffled his hair. "Next time, take me with you!"

The boys laughed, already imagining their next underwater expedition. They knew that the ocean held more secrets, and they were determined to uncover every one of them.

As the sun set on their village, painting the sky with hues of pink and orange, Tommy and Max stood by the water's edge, gazing out at the sea. There were more adventures to be had, more treasures to discover, and more mysteries to solve.

"This is only the beginning," Tommy said, clutching the new map tightly.

Max nodded. "Let's see where it takes us."

And with that, the two best friends—now seasoned treasure hunters—prepared for the next chapter of their great underwater adventure.

Die Große Unterwasserschatzsuche

Tommy und Max waren schon immer die besten Freunde. Sie lebten in einem Küstendorf, wo die salzige Brise den Duft von Abenteuern trug und ihre Fantasie so wild war wie die tosenden Wellen. Jeden Tag nach der Schule trafen sie sich am Strand und träumten von den verborgenen Geheimnissen unter dem Meer.

Eines Samstagmorgens geschah etwas Außergewöhnliches, das ihre wildesten Träume Wirklichkeit werden ließ.

Die Entdeckung

Es war ein heller, sonniger Tag, als Tommy und Max loszogen, um die Gezeitenbecken in der Nähe der Felsklippen zu erkunden. Das hatten sie schon hundertmal gemacht, auf der Suche nach Krabben, glänzenden Muscheln und winzigen Fischen, aber heute fühlte es sich anders an. Als sie über die glitschigen Felsen kletterten, stieß Tommy mit seinem Fuß gegen etwas Hartes.

„Aua!", schrie Tommy und rieb sich den Fuß.

„Was ist das?", fragte Max und deutete auf den glänzenden Gegenstand, der halb im Sand vergraben war.

Tommy hockte sich hin und grub ihn aus. Es war eine alte, verrostete Metallkiste. Die Scharniere knarrten, und die

Oberfläche war mit seltsamen Markierungen bedeckt. Max' Augen weiteten sich, als Tommy vorsichtig die Kiste öffnete.

Drinnen fanden sie ein zusammengerolltes Pergament, vergilbt vom Alter. Max rollte es auf, und ihre Herzen schlugen schneller. Es war eine alte Schatzkarte! Die Markierungen sahen aus, als wären sie Jahrhunderte alt, und die Karte zeigte eine Route weit hinaus ins Meer, markiert mit einem großen „X".

„Tommy, weißt du, was das bedeutet?", flüsterte Max, seine Stimme zitterte vor Aufregung.

Tommy grinste. „Es bedeutet, dass wir auf Schatzsuche gehen!"

Die Planung des Abenteuers

An diesem Nachmittag trafen sich die Jungs in ihrem geheimen Clubhaus – einem Baumhaus in Tommys Garten. Sie breiteten die Karte auf dem Boden aus und untersuchten jedes Detail. Die Route begann an ihrem Dorfsstrand und erstreckte sich weit ins tiefblaue Meer, vorbei an einem Korallenriff und einer Unterwasserhöhle.

„Wir werden Tauchausrüstung brauchen", sagte Max.

„Und ein Boot!", fügte Tommy hinzu.

Zum Glück hatte Tommys Vater ein kleines Fischerboot, und Max' ältere Schwester arbeitete im örtlichen Tauchladen. Die Jungs verbrachten den Rest des Tages damit, sich auf ihr großes Abenteuer vorzubereiten. Sie liehen sich Tauchanzüge, Schnorchel und packten ihre Taschen mit Snacks und Ausrüstung.

Als die Sonne unterging, waren sie bereit.

„Wir brechen im Morgengrauen auf", sagte Tommy, seine Stimme vor Vorfreude zitternd.

Max nickte. „Morgen finden wir den Schatz."

In See stechen

Am nächsten Morgen, bei den ersten Sonnenstrahlen, luden Tommy und Max ihre Ausrüstung auf das kleine Boot und machten sich auf den Weg. Das Wasser schimmerte wie flüssiges Gold unter der aufgehenden Sonne, und die Jungs spürten, wie die Aufregung in ihnen aufstieg.

Sie folgten der Route der Karte und navigierten die Küste entlang, bis sie das Korallenriff erreichten. Bunt schillernde Fische schwammen unter ihnen, huschten zwischen den Felsen und Korallen hindurch. Das Riff war atemberaubend, aber die Jungs hatten etwas viel Größeres im Kopf: den Schatz.

„Laut der Karte ist der Eingang zur Unterwasserhöhle direkt hinter dem Riff", sagte Tommy und kniff die Augen zusammen, um das Pergament zu lesen.

Max spähte in die Ferne. „Da! Ich sehe ihn!" Er zeigte auf eine dunkle Form unter der Wasseroberfläche.

Sie ließen den Anker fallen und zogen ihre Tauchausrüstung an. Mit klopfenden Herzen tauchten die Jungs ins kühle Wasser. Während sie hinabtauchten, verschwand die Welt über ihnen und wurde durch ein magisches Unterwasserkönigreich ersetzt.

Die Unterwasserhöhle

Der Eingang zur Höhle war riesig, ein klaffendes Maul im Meeresboden. Die Jungs schwammen hinein, ihre Taschenlampen schnitten durch die Dunkelheit. Die Höhle war unheimlich, aber wunderschön. Glitzernde Steine bedeckten die Wände, und seltsame Meereskreaturen spähten aus versteckten Nischen hervor.

Tommy zeigte nach vorne. „Da ist es – das 'X'!"

In der Mitte der Höhle, in den Felsenboden eingraviert, war ein riesiges „X", genau wie auf der Karte.

Max' Augen weiteten sich. „Das ist es!"

Sie schwammen hinunter zum „X" und begannen nach Hinweisen zu suchen. Max' Hand streifte etwas Metallisches. Er räumte den Sand weg und enthüllte eine große, alte Truhe, die mit Seepocken bedeckt war.

„Hilf mir, sie hochzuheben!", rief Max, seine Stimme voll Aufregung und Anstrengung.

Gemeinsam hievten sie die Truhe aus dem Sand. Sie war schwer, aber das Versprechen dessen, was drinnen lag, beflügelte ihre Kräfte. Tommy öffnete die Truhe mit einem Brecheisen, und ihre Augen weiteten sich, als sie den Inhalt sahen.

Der Schatz

Die Truhe war gefüllt mit funkelnden Goldmünzen, glitzernden Juwelen und kunstvoll geschnitzten Statuen. Es gab alte Relikte verlorener Zivilisationen und sogar eine mit Diamanten besetzte Krone. Es war mehr Schatz, als sie sich jemals hätten vorstellen können.

„Wir sind reich!", rief Tommy, seine Stimme sprudelte durch den Schnorchel.

Max lachte. „Das ist unglaublich! Wir haben wirklich einen versteckten Schatz gefunden!"

Aber als sie ihren Fund bewunderten, bemerkten sie etwas anderes am Boden der Truhe – ein zusammengerolltes Pergament, ähnlich der Karte, die sie zuvor gefunden hatten. Max rollte es auf, und die Jungs starrten ungläubig.

Es war eine weitere Schatzkarte.

„Aber diese führt noch weiter weg", sagte Tommy und untersuchte die neue Karte. Sie zeigte eine Route, die noch tiefer ins Meer führte, zu einem Ort, den sie noch nie gesehen hatten.

Max grinste. „Sieht so aus, als wäre unser Abenteuer noch nicht zu Ende."

Die große Rückkehr

Nachdem sie mitgenommen hatten, was sie tragen konnten, kehrten die Jungs zu ihrem Boot zurück, die Herzen voller Aufregung. Während sie zurück zum Ufer segelten, konnten sie nicht aufhören zu grinsen. Sie hatten echten Schatz gefunden, und das Abenteuer ihres Lebens war noch nicht vorbei.

Als sie den Strand erreichten, erzählten sie ihren Familien ihre Geschichte. Natürlich glaubten die Erwachsenen ihnen zunächst nicht – bis sie die funkelnden Goldmünzen und Juwelen sahen.

Tommys Vater hob eine Augenbraue. „Ihr Jungs versteht es wirklich, Ärger zu finden", sagte er lächelnd. „Aber es sieht so aus, als hättet ihr auch das Abenteuer eures Lebens gefunden."

Max' Schwester wuschelte ihm durchs Haar. „Nächstes Mal nehmt ihr mich mit!"

Die Jungs lachten und stellten sich schon ihr nächstes Unterwasserabenteuer vor. Sie wussten, dass das Meer noch mehr Geheimnisse barg, und sie waren entschlossen, jedes einzelne davon zu lüften.

Als die Sonne über ihrem Dorf unterging und den Himmel in Rosa und Orange tauchte, standen Tommy und Max am Wasser und blickten aufs Meer hinaus. Es gab noch mehr Abenteuer zu erleben, noch mehr Schätze zu entdecken und noch mehr Geheimnisse zu lösen.

„Das ist erst der Anfang", sagte Tommy und hielt die neue Karte fest in der Hand.

Max nickte. „Mal sehen, wohin sie uns führt."

Und damit bereiteten sich die beiden besten Freunde – jetzt erfahrene Schatzsucher – auf das nächste Kapitel ihres großen Unterwasserabenteuers vor.

The Cat with a Thousand Lives

In the sleepy little town of Willowbrook, there was a legend—one whispered among children and passed down through generations. It was the tale of a mysterious cat, a magical feline who had lived for hundreds of years. Some said it had a thousand lives, always appearing when someone needed it most. Its name was simply *Luna*.

Most thought the story was just an old town myth. But those who had seen Luna knew better.

A Strange Visitor

On a crisp autumn morning, young Emily was sitting on her front porch, watching the golden leaves flutter down from the trees. It had been a tough week. Her dad had lost his job, and the town's bakery, which her mom owned, was struggling to stay open. Emily had overheard her parents whispering late into the night, worried about the future.

Just as she let out a long sigh, something caught her eye. A sleek black cat, with fur as dark as midnight and eyes that shimmered like silver moons, appeared at the edge of her yard. It padded silently toward her, its tail curling in the air like a question mark.

"Hello there," Emily said softly, kneeling down.

The cat, without hesitation, rubbed against her legs and purred loudly. Emily had never seen a cat like it before, but something about the animal felt familiar—almost comforting.

"Where did you come from?" she asked, petting its silky fur.

The cat blinked slowly at her, as if to say, *You'll see*.

The First Miracle

That afternoon, Emily's mom, Mrs. Blake, was preparing for what could be the bakery's last chance—a big town festival where she hoped to sell enough pies and bread to keep the business alive. But there was a problem. The oven, an old, creaky thing, had broken down, and no one in town had the parts to fix it.

As Mrs. Blake sat in the kitchen, her head in her hands, Emily noticed the black cat—Luna—slinking through the open door. Luna hopped up onto the kitchen counter and stared at the broken oven. She walked over to the appliance and, with a gentle nudge of her paw, pressed a button.

Suddenly, the oven roared back to life, glowing with warmth. Mrs. Blake gasped.

"What on earth...?" she muttered, staring at the oven in disbelief.

Emily smiled knowingly. "I think Luna's here to help."

Her mom shook her head, still baffled. "Well, whatever it was, we're back in business."

With the oven fixed, Mrs. Blake baked into the night, filling the kitchen with the sweet scent of pies, bread, and cakes. Luna curled up on the windowsill, watching silently.

The Second Miracle

A few days later, the festival was in full swing. The bakery stall was set up, but there was another problem. The delivery van that was supposed to bring flour and sugar from the next town had broken down. Without more supplies, they wouldn't be able to keep up with demand.

As Mrs. Blake anxiously made calls, Emily noticed Luna had disappeared. She searched the festival grounds, calling out for the cat, but there was no sign of her.

Just as Emily was about to give up, she heard a faint meowing. Luna was sitting in the back of an old pickup truck, parked near the edge of the festival. Emily ran over to her, curious.

"Luna? What are you doing here?"

At that moment, the truck's owner—Mr. Phelps, a kind farmer from the next town over—approached. He smiled at Emily.

"Looks like your cat found me. I heard about your supply problem, and I just happened to have extra flour and sugar with me. I'll drop it off at your stall right away."

Emily beamed. "Thank you so much, Mr. Phelps!"

As the farmer loaded up their supplies, Emily scratched Luna's head. "You really do always show up at the perfect time, don't you?"

Luna purred in response.

The Final Miracle

By the end of the festival, the bakery had done better than Mrs. Blake had hoped. They had sold out of nearly everything, and it looked like the bakery would be saved after all. Emily and her family were overjoyed.

But as the festival was winding down, a commotion stirred near the park. A large crowd had gathered, and Emily could hear someone shouting for help.

She rushed over and saw that a young boy had climbed up into a tree to retrieve his kite, but now he was stuck. The boy clung to a high branch, too scared to come down, and no one could reach him.

Before anyone could call for help, Luna darted through the crowd, her black fur a blur as she raced toward the tree. In one graceful leap, she climbed up the trunk with incredible speed and balance.

The crowd watched in astonishment as Luna reached the boy. She rubbed against his arm and meowed softly, giving him the courage he needed to move. Slowly but surely, the boy began to make his way down, with Luna leading the way. Step by step, the crowd held its breath until finally, the boy reached the ground safely.

The crowd erupted into cheers, and the boy's parents scooped him up into their arms.

Emily smiled, her heart swelling with pride. "You did it again, Luna," she whispered.

But when she looked around, Luna was nowhere to be seen. The cat had disappeared into the shadows, as if she had never been there at all.

A Thousand Lives

As the days passed, life in Willowbrook returned to normal. The bakery thrived, thanks to the success of the festival, and Emily's dad found a new job that he loved. Everything seemed to be falling into place.

But Emily never forgot about Luna. She knew the cat wasn't just any ordinary feline. Luna had been there for her family when they needed her most—just like in the town legends. And even though Luna had vanished, Emily felt certain the magical cat would return when the time was right.

Because, after all, Luna had a thousand lives. And each one was dedicated to saving the day, just when someone needed her the most.

Die Katze mit den Tausend Leben

In der verschlafenen kleinen Stadt Willowbrook gab es eine Legende – eine, die unter Kindern geflüstert und über Generationen hinweg erzählt wurde. Es war die Geschichte von einer geheimnisvollen Katze, einem magischen Tier, das seit Hunderten von Jahren lebte. Einige sagten, sie hätte tausend Leben und tauche immer dann auf, wenn sie am meisten gebraucht würde. Ihr Name war schlicht Luna.

Die meisten dachten, die Geschichte sei nur ein alter Stadtmythos. Aber diejenigen, die Luna gesehen hatten, wussten es besser.

Ein seltsamer Besucher

An einem frischen Herbstmorgen saß die junge Emily auf ihrer Veranda und beobachtete, wie die goldenen Blätter von den Bäumen flatterten. Es war eine schwierige Woche gewesen. Ihr Vater hatte seinen Job verloren, und die Bäckerei ihrer Mutter, die einzige in der Stadt, kämpfte ums Überleben. Emily hatte ihre Eltern spät in der Nacht flüstern hören, besorgt über die Zukunft.

Gerade als sie einen langen Seufzer ausstieß, erregte etwas ihre Aufmerksamkeit. Eine schlanke schwarze Katze, deren Fell so dunkel wie die Mitternacht war und deren Augen wie silberne Monde schimmerten, erschien am Rand ihres Gartens. Lautlos schlich sie auf Emily zu, ihr Schwanz in der Luft gekrümmt wie ein Fragezeichen.

„Hallo", sagte Emily leise und kniete sich hin.

Die Katze zögerte nicht und rieb sich schnurrend an ihren Beinen. Emily hatte noch nie eine Katze wie diese gesehen, aber irgendetwas an ihr kam ihr vertraut vor – fast tröstlich.

„Wo kommst du her?" fragte sie, während sie das seidige Fell der Katze streichelte.

Die Katze blinzelte langsam, als wollte sie sagen: *Du wirst es sehen.*

Das erste Wunder

An diesem Nachmittag bereitete Emilys Mutter, Frau Blake, sich auf das vielleicht letzte große Ereignis der Bäckerei vor – ein großes Stadtfest, auf dem sie hoffte, genügend Kuchen und Brot zu verkaufen, um das Geschäft zu retten. Doch es gab ein Problem. Der Ofen, ein altes, klappriges Ding, war kaputtgegangen, und niemand in der Stadt hatte die Ersatzteile, um ihn zu reparieren.

Während Frau Blake in der Küche saß und den Kopf in die Hände stützte, bemerkte Emily die schwarze Katze – Luna –, die durch die offene Tür schlich. Luna sprang auf die Küchenarbeitsplatte und starrte den kaputten Ofen an. Sie ging zu dem Gerät hinüber und drückte mit einer sanften Pfote einen Knopf.

Plötzlich erwachte der Ofen wieder zum Leben und strahlte eine warme Hitze aus. Frau Blake schnappte nach Luft.

„Was in aller Welt...?" murmelte sie und starrte den Ofen ungläubig an.

Emily lächelte wissend. „Ich glaube, Luna ist hier, um zu helfen."

Ihre Mutter schüttelte den Kopf, immer noch verwundert. „Nun, was auch immer es war, wir können weitermachen."

Mit dem reparierten Ofen backte Frau Blake die ganze Nacht hindurch und füllte die Küche mit dem süßen Duft von Kuchen, Brot und Torten. Luna rollte sich auf der Fensterbank zusammen und beobachtete alles still.

Das zweite Wunder

Ein paar Tage später war das Stadtfest in vollem Gange. Der Stand der Bäckerei war aufgebaut, doch es gab erneut ein Problem. Der Lieferwagen, der Mehl und Zucker aus der Nachbarstadt bringen sollte, war kaputtgegangen. Ohne Nachschub konnten sie die Nachfrage nicht bedienen.

Während Frau Blake besorgt telefonierte, bemerkte Emily, dass Luna verschwunden war. Sie durchsuchte das Festgelände und rief nach der Katze, aber sie war nirgends zu finden.

Gerade als Emily aufgeben wollte, hörte sie ein leises Miauen. Luna saß auf der Ladefläche eines alten Pick-up-Trucks, der am Rande des Festgeländes geparkt war. Emily rannte zu ihr, neugierig.

„Luna? Was machst du hier?"

In diesem Moment kam der Besitzer des Trucks – Herr Phelps, ein freundlicher Bauer aus der Nachbarstadt – auf sie zu. Er lächelte Emily an.

„Sieht so aus, als hätte deine Katze mich gefunden. Ich habe von eurem Problem mit den Vorräten gehört und zufällig extra Mehl und Zucker dabei. Ich bringe es gleich zu eurem Stand."

Emily strahlte. „Vielen Dank, Herr Phelps!"

Während der Bauer die Vorräte ablieferte, kratzte Emily Luna hinter den Ohren. „Du tauchst wirklich immer genau zum richtigen Zeitpunkt auf, oder?"

Luna schnurrte als Antwort.

Das letzte Wunder

Am Ende des Festes hatte die Bäckerei besser abgeschnitten, als Frau Blake es je gehofft hatte. Fast alles war ausverkauft, und es sah so aus, als sei die Bäckerei gerettet. Emily und ihre Familie waren überglücklich.

Doch als das Fest zu Ende ging, entstand ein Aufruhr im Park. Eine große Menschenmenge hatte sich versammelt, und Emily hörte jemanden um Hilfe rufen.

Sie rannte hin und sah, dass ein kleiner Junge auf einen Baum geklettert war, um seinen Drachen zu holen, aber jetzt saß er fest. Der Junge klammerte sich an einen hohen Ast und hatte zu viel

Angst, um wieder herunterzuklettern, und niemand konnte ihn erreichen.

Noch bevor jemand um Hilfe rufen konnte, rannte Luna durch die Menge, ihr schwarzes Fell ein verschwommener Streifen, als sie zum Baum raste. Mit einem eleganten Sprung kletterte sie den Stamm hinauf, mit unglaublicher Geschwindigkeit und Balance.

Die Menge sah erstaunt zu, wie Luna den Jungen erreichte. Sie rieb sich an seinem Arm und miaute sanft, gab ihm den Mut, sich zu bewegen. Langsam, aber sicher, begann der Junge, den Baum hinunterzuklettern, mit Luna an seiner Seite. Schritt für Schritt hielt die Menge den Atem an, bis der Junge endlich sicher den Boden erreichte.

Die Menge brach in Jubel aus, und die Eltern des Jungen schlossen ihn in die Arme.

Emily lächelte, ihr Herz war erfüllt von Stolz. „Du hast es wieder geschafft, Luna", flüsterte sie.

Aber als sie sich umsah, war Luna nirgends zu sehen. Die Katze war in die Schatten verschwunden, als wäre sie nie dort gewesen.

Tausend Leben

Als die Tage vergingen, kehrte das Leben in Willowbrook zur Normalität zurück. Die Bäckerei florierte dank des Erfolgs des Festes, und Emilys Vater fand einen neuen Job, den er liebte. Alles schien sich zum Besseren zu wenden.

Doch Emily vergaß Luna nie. Sie wusste, dass die Katze nicht einfach irgendeine gewöhnliche Katze war. Luna war für ihre Familie da gewesen, als sie sie am meisten brauchten – genau wie in den Legenden der Stadt. Und obwohl Luna verschwunden war, war sich Emily sicher, dass die magische Katze zurückkehren würde, wenn die Zeit reif war.

Denn schließlich hatte Luna tausend Leben. Und jedes einzelne davon war dazu bestimmt, den Tag zu retten, genau dann, wenn sie am dringendsten gebraucht wurde.